P9-CJC-300

DATE DUE

AP 24 '00			

DEMCO 38-296

FRENCH
ART SONGS
OF THE NINETEENTH CENTURY
39 Works from Berlioz to Debussy

R

FRENCH ART SONGS

OF THE NINETEENTH CENTURY

39 Works from Berlioz to Debussy

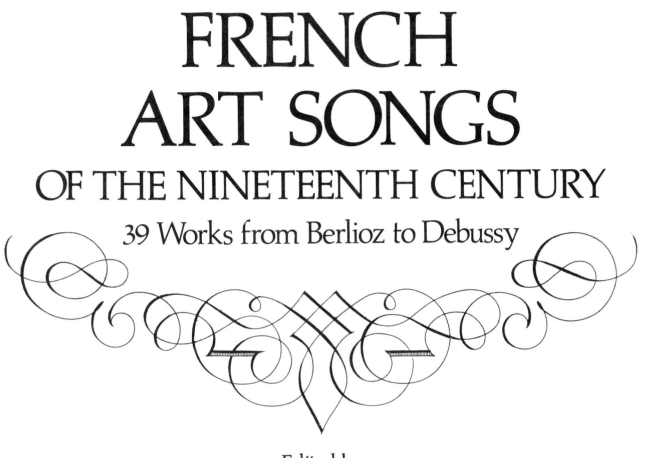

Edited by

Philip Hale

Dover Publications, Inc.

New York

Riverside Community College

OCT '98

4800 Magnolia Avenue
Riverside, CA 92506

M 1730 .F74 1978

French art songs of the
 nineteenth century

Copyright © 1904 by Oliver Ditson Company.
All rights reserved under Pan American
and International Copyright Conventions.

Published in Canada by General Publishing Company, Ltd.,
30 Lesmill Road, Don Mills, Toronto, Ontario.
Published in the United Kingdom by Constable and
Company, Ltd.

This Dover edition, first published in 1978, is a new selec-
tion of songs from the two-volume set ("Bemberg to
Franck" and "Georges to Widor") originally published by
the Oliver Ditson Company, Boston, 1904, under the title
Modern French Songs (for High Voice) in the series "The
Musicians Library." The present edition is published by
special arrangement with the Theodore Presser Company,
Bryn Mawr, Pennsylvania.

International Standard Book Number: 0-486-23680-3
Library of Congress Catalog Card Number: 78-53252

Manufactured in the United States of America
Dover Publications, Inc.
180 Varick Street
New York, N.Y. 10014

CONTENTS

Dates of birth and death of composers and poets, as well as dates of composition and other information, have been completed and corrected wherever possible in this 1978 edition. Only the French song titles are given here.

à Mademoiselle Wolf

VILLANELLE

(Original Key)

THÉOPHILE GAUTIER
Translated by Isabella G. Parker

HECTOR BERLIOZ

When shall come Spring's de-light-ful weath-er, When bleak Win-ter hath passed a-way,

Quand vien-dra la sai-son nou-vel-le, Quand au-ront dis-pa-ru les froids,

Then, my love, we will go to-geth-er, Gath-'ring lil-ies in wood-land gay.

Tous les deux nous i-rons, ma bel-le, Pour cueil-lir le mu-guet aux bois.

Pearls _____ of dew from our foot - steps
Sous _____ nos pieds é - gre - nant les

fling - ing, Trem - bling bright in the morn - ing ray, _____
per - les Que l'on voit au ma - tin trem - bler, _____

Then will we hear the black-birds sing-ing,
Nous i - rons é - cou - ter les mer - les,

Then will we hear the black-birds sing - ing, All day!
Nous i - rons é - cou - ter les mer - les Sif - fler.

Spring is come, O my love, so bright - ly;
Le prin - temps est ve - nu, ma bel - le,

'Tis the month for all lov - ers blest:_____
C'est le mois des a - mants bé - ni;_____

Bird - ling, poised on his wing so light - ly,
Et l'oi - seau, sa - ti - nant son ai - le,

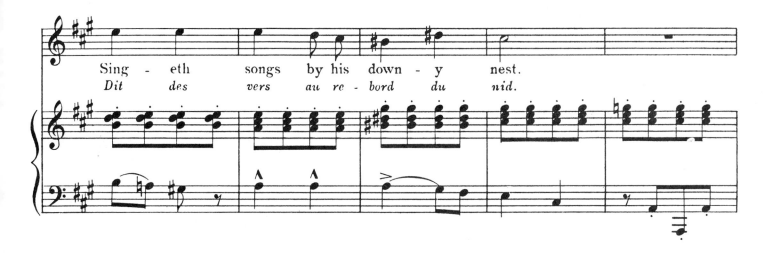

Sing - eth songs by his down - y nest.
Dit des vers au re - bord du nid.

Oh, come. On moss-y bank re - pos - ing,
Oh! Viens donc sur ce banc de mous - se

We will talk of our love to - day,_____
Pour par - ler de nos beaux a - mours,_____

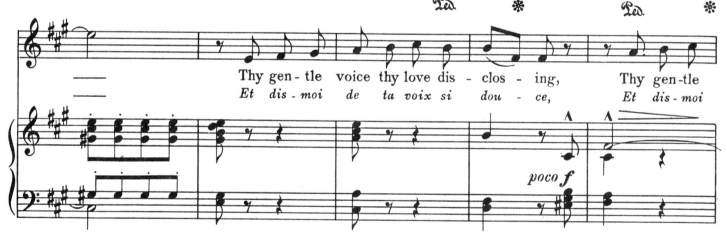

Thy gen - tle voice thy love dis - clos - ing, Thy gen-tle
Et dis - moi de ta voix si dou - ce, Et dis - moi

voice thy love dis - clos - ing Al - way!
de ta voix si dou - ce: Tou - jours!

Far a-way
Loin, bien loin

through the wood we'll wan-der, Fright the hare, hid-ing as we pass,___
é - ga-rant nos cour-ses, Fai - sons fuir le la-pin ca - ché___

Where the deer sees his ant - lers yon - der,
Et le daim, au mi - roir des sour - ces

mf

senza accel.
(sans presser)

Mir - rored fair in the spring's clear glass; Then
Ad - mi - rant son grand bois pen - ché; Puis

p

a - - lone in our syl - van pleas - ures, Fin - gers twin - ing, the
chez nous, tout heu - reux, tout ai - ses, En pa - niers en - la -

while we roam,_____ We'll from the
çant nos doigts,_____ Re - ve - nons,

wood its fruit - y treas - ures, We'll from the wood its fruit-y treasures Bring home.
rap - por - tant des frai - ses, Re - ve - nons, rap- por-tant des frai - ses Des bois!

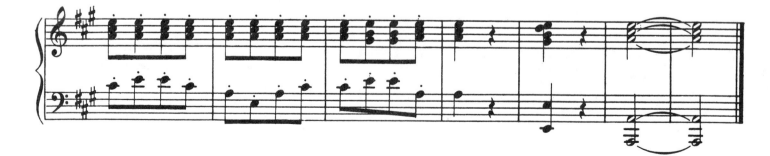

A Mme. Miolan-Carvalho

IN THE WOODS
(VIEILLE CHANSON)
(Original Key)

CHARLES H. MILLEVOYE
Translated by Isabella G. Parker

GEORGES BIZET

In the woods am - o - rous Myr -
Dans les bois l'a - mou - reux Myr -

til Caught a lin - net sing - ing so clear - ly,
til A - vait pris fau - vet - te lé - gè - re

"Thou love - ly bird, ___ fear thou no ill, For my true
Ai - ma - ble oi - seau ___ lui di - sait - il: Je te des -

love will love thee dear - ly. _____ And in re-
tine à ma ber gè - re _____ *Pour prix du*

turn _____ for thee to - day _____ With kiss - es
don _____ *que j'au - rai fait* _____ *Que de bai -*

sweet _____ she will re - pay. _____ If my be - lov - ed
sers, _____ *que de bai - sers!* _____ *Si ma Lu - cet - te,*

gave so de - mure - ly Two kiss - es for a bright bou -
si ma Lu - cet - te *M'en don - ne deux pour un bou -*

quet__ She'll give me ten,__ she'll give me ten, ah!_____
quet__ J'en au-rai dix,__ j'en au-rai dix, ah!_____

__ She'll give me ten for thee most sure - ly."
__ J'en au-rai dix pour la fau-vet - te.

But the bird - ling had left her
La fau-vet - te dans le val-

mate,__ And his love - song she heard out - pour - ing So a -
lon__ A lais - sé son a - mi fi - dè - le Et tant

las,   a - las,   a - las,   Myr - til saw too
fait,   *tant fait,*   *tant fait,*   *que de sa pri -*

late, His cap - tive far on swift wing soar - ing.
son El - le s'é - chappe à ti - re d'ai - le.

"Ah," said the shep-herd in dis - may, _____ A - dieu to kiss - es from my
Ah! dit le ber - ger dé - so - lé _____ *A - dieu les bai - sers de Lu -*

treas - ure! All my de - light _____ is flown a - way With the
cet - te! Tout mon bon - heur _____ *s'est en - vo - lé* _____ *Sur les*

bird, gone— is all my pleas-ure!" The shep - herd sad - ly wan-der'd
ai - les— de la fau - vet-te! Myr - til re - tour - ne au bois voi -

home,— With sor - row dark-ly brood-ing o'er—
sin — Pleu - rant la per - te qu'il a fai - -

him. But see Myr - til what joy is come! In the
te Soit par ha - sard, soit à des - sein, Dans le

path stands his love be - fore— him! Then how lov-ing-ly his
bois se trou - vait Lu - cet - te; Et sen - si - ble à ce

faith-ful Lu-cette Ad-vanc-es to her shep-herd lonely And smil-ing
ga - ge de foi— El - le sor-tit de sa re - traite En lui di -

appassionato e cresc.

says: "Do not re - gret, do not re-gret, Myr-til,— do not re-
sant: Con - so - le - toi, Con - so - le - toi, Myr - til,— con - so - le -

appassionato e cresc. *rall.*

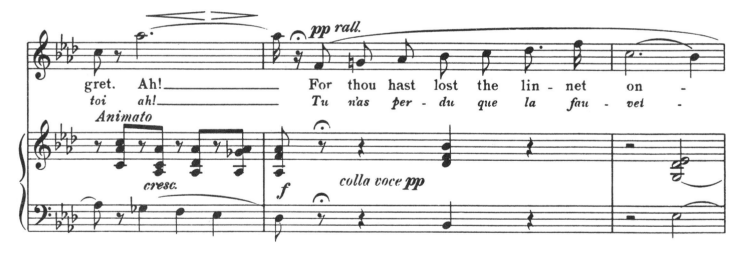

gret. Ah!———————— For thou hast lost the lin - net on -
toi ah!———————— Tu n'as per - du que la fau - vet -

Animato

cresc. *f* *colla voce pp*

ly."
te.

p a tempo *p*

A Mme. Ernest Bertrand

PASTORAL
(PASTORALE)
(Original Key)

J. F. REGNARD
English version by Isabella G. Parker

GEORGES BIZET

In Spring-time one day___
Un jour___ de prin - temps,___

Through a gar-den most fair___
Tout le long d'un ver - ger___

Sang Co - lin this lay___
Co - lin va chan - tant,___

To be-guile his de - spair:___ "Maid-en dear-est, maid-en dear-est,—
Pour ses maux sou - la - ger:___ "Ma ber - gè - re, ma ber - gè - re,

tra la la la la la la la la,___ Maid-en dear-est, maid-en dear-est,
tra la la la la la la la la,___ Ma ber-gè-re, ma ber-gè-re,

poco sf espress. *poco - -*

tra la la la la la la la la,___ Tell me now, tell me now,-
tra la la la la la la la la,___ Lais-se-moi, lais-se-moi

poco sf *suivez - -*

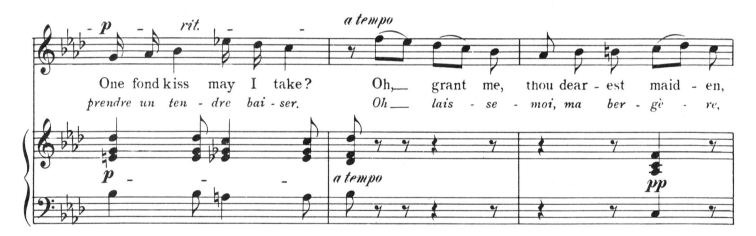

-p *-rit.* *a tempo*

One fond kiss may I take? Oh,___ grant me, thou dear-est maid-en,
prendre un ten-dre bai-ser. *Oh___ lais-se-moi, ma ber-gè-re,*

p *a tempo*

pp

rit. molto *a tempo* *con anima*

grant me one ten-der kiss._____ O thou maid-en
prendre un ten-dre bai-ser._____ Ma ber-gè-

a tempo

colla voce *mf*

Ped. *

dear, Give___ me,___ I pray___ thee, one ten -
re lais - se - moi pren - - dre un ten -

- - - der kiss?-
- - dre bai - ser!"-

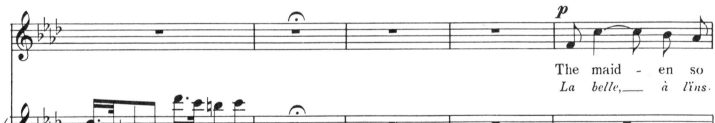

The maid - en so
La belle,___ à l'ins-

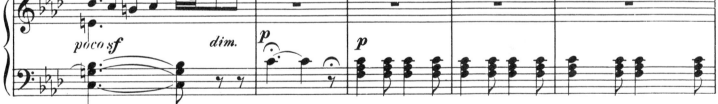

bright _____
tant_____

An-swered Co - lin with
Ré-pond à son ber -

this :— "Will you, sing-ing light,
ger :— "Tu veux, en chan - tant,

Will you steal a fond kiss?— No, Co - lin,— no, Co - lin,
Un bai - ser dé - ro - ber?— Non Co - lin,— non Co - lin,

tra la la la la la la la la, No, Co - lin,— no, Co - lin,
tra la la la la la la la la— Non Co - lin,— non Co - lin,

tra la la la la la la la la;— Would you then, while you sing,
tra la la la la la la la la,— Tu vou - drais, en' chan - tant;

Steal a fond kiss from me? No, no, no, no, Co - lin, take it not;
prendre un ten - dre bai - ser? Non, non, non, non, Co - lin, ne le prends pas,

I will give it to thee! No, no, no, Co -
Je vais te le don - ner! Non, non, non, Co -

lin, no, take it not; I will give it to
lin, ne le prends pas, Je vais te le don -

thee!
ner!"

WERE I GARDENER
(SI J'ÉTAIS JARDINIER)

ROGER MILES

Translated by Isabella G. Parker

CÉCILE CHAMINADE

When the pale shad - ows veil thee night - ly. Thou should'st beam in glo - ry on
Dans la nuit pâ - le sous ses voi - les Ton é - clat se - rait ra - di -

high. Were I gard - 'ner of the sky Stars for thee I'd
eux. Si j'é - tais jar - di - nier des cieux Je te cueil - le -

cull, gleam-ing bright - ly!
rais des é - toi - les!

Or if gard-'ner of Love I were, With ca-ress-es I___ would de-
Si j'é-tais jar-di-nier d'a-mour Je te cueil-le-rais___ des ca-

light thee. All the day would I feast thee, dear. If the gard'ner of
res-ses, Je te fê-te-rais tout le jour Si j'é-tais jar-di-

rit.   *a tempo*

Love I were! Flowers with voice-less charm should in-vite thee
nier d'a-mour! En___ leurs i-né-di-tes ten-dres-ses

And in low-ly hom-age ap-pear. If the gard'ner of Love I were,
Mes bouquets te fe-raient la cour. Si j'é-tais jar-di-nier d'a-mour

With ca - ress - es   I   would de - light ____ thee!
Je   te cueil-le - rais des ca - res - ses!

My gar-den hath no flower but   song; ____
Mais mon jar - din n'est que chan - sons, ____

To thee a - lone that flower is   giv - en.
Et   tu peux y cueil - lir toi - mê - me,

The birds with - in the thick - et ___ throng, ____
Dieu pour les   nids fit les buis - sons ____

à Mlle. Marie Veyssier

IF THOU SHOULDST TELL ME
(TU ME DIRAIS)

(Original Key)

ROSEMONDE GÉRARD
Translated by Isabella G. Parker

CÉCILE CHAMINADE

night.____ If thou should'st tell me all my verse is pro - sy— 'Tis safe with
lon,____ Tu me di - rais que ces vers sont en pro - se, Et qu'u - ne

wom - an a se - cret to leave— That lil - ies speak, and that the blue is
femme a gar - dé des se - crets, Que le lys parle et que l'a - zur est

ro - sy, So fool - ish I, my love, I should be - lieve. If thou should'st
ro - se, Vois ma fo - lie, a - mi, je te croi - rais. Tu me di -

tell me ev - 'ry star is spar-kling With beams the glow-worm lends to make it
rais que l'as - tre qui scin - til - le, Au ver lui - sant doit son é - clat joy-

bright,____ And that the night doth pin her man-tle dark -iing Like jew - el
eux,____ *Et que la nuit ac-croche à sa man - til - le,* *Comme un bi-*

fair with the sun's ra-diant light._____ If thou should'st
jou le so - leil ra - di - eux;_____ *Tu me di -*

tell me no red fruit is grow-ing.— The moss-y nooks of the wood but de-
rais qu'il n'est plus u - ne frai - se *Dans les re - coins tout mous-sus des fo -*

ceive.— That light-er than the light-est feath - er blow - ing__ My grief doth
rêts, *Et qu'u - ne plu - me de ben-ga - li pè - se__ Plus qu'un cha-*

à Mademoiselle Fanny Lépine

THE DEAD
(LES MORTS)

(Original Key)

JEAN RICHEPIN
Translated by Isabella G. Parker

ERNEST CHAUSSON

When at eve the bright sun is set, You have but your eye-lids to close.
Lors - que le so - leil s'est cou - ché, Tu n'as qu'a fer - mer tes deux yeux

When he is ris - en, bright once more.____
Pour qu'il s'y lè - ve, ral - lu - mé.____

The bird flies on-ward, The bird is gone;____ Yet while he is
L'oi-seau s'en - vo - le, l'oi-seau s'en va;____ Mais pen-dant qu'il

hov - 'ring on high, His shad - ow on the earth re - main -
pla - ne là - haut, Son om - bre res - te sur la ter -

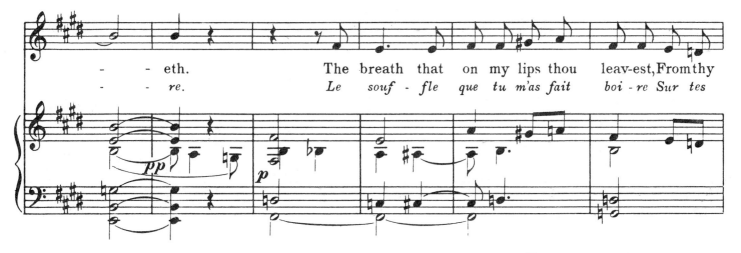

- -eth. The breath that on my lips thou leav-est, From thy
- -re. _Le souf - fle que tu m'as fait boi - re Sur tes_

own lips,____ in go - ing forth,____ It is my own,____
_lè - vres,____ en t'en al - lant,____ Il est en moi,_____

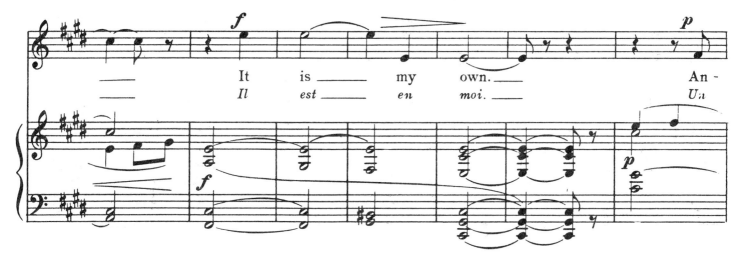

It is____ my own.____ An -
_Il est____ en moi.____ U:1_

oth-er it to thee hath given, in go - ing forth.
au - tre te l'a - vait don - né en s'en al - lant,

In go-ing forth I will give it then to an - oth - er. ___
En m'en al - lant, je le don - ne-rai à un au - tre.

From lip to lip ___ it pass-eth on; From lip to
De bouche en bouche ___ il a pas - sé; De bouche en

lip ___ 'Twill pass a - long. And thus ___ can
bouche ___ il pas - se - ra. Ain - si ___ ja -

ne'er, ___ can ne'er be lost. ___
mais ___ ne se per - dra. ___

THE BELLS
(LES CLOCHES)

(Original Key)

PAUL BOURGET
Translated by Isabella G. Parker

CLAUDE DEBUSSY

warn - - ing, A - far through the air, Bring - ing mem - 'ry
en - - ne, Ce loin - tain ap - pel Me re - mé - mo -

rit. e dim.

sweet of lil - ies a - dorn - - ing Ho - ly al - tar
rait la blan - cheur chré - tien - ne Des fleurs de l'au -

rit. e dim.

fair.
tel.

poco meno mosso
(un peu plus lent)

p

dolce ed espress.
(doux et expressif)
p

These bells tell of hap - py years now o'er -
Ces clo - ches par - laient d'heu - reu - ses an -

shad - - ed, And with sol - emn
né - - es, Et dans le grand

tone. Once more they re - fresh the leaves that are
bois Sem - blaient re - ver - dir les feuil - les - fa -

cresc.

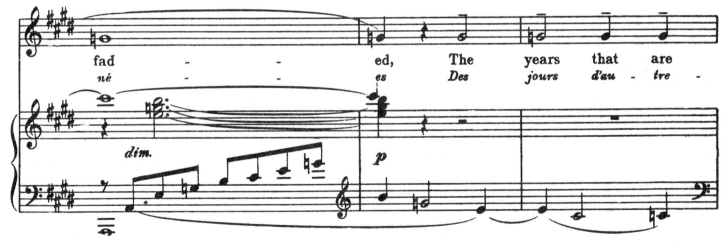

fad - - ed, The years that are
né - - es Des jours d'au - tre -

dim. p

gone.
fois.
a tempo

R.H.

pp

ppp

L.H.

THE TEARS FALL IN MY SOUL
(IL PLEURE DANS MON CŒUR)

PAUL VERLAINE
Translated by Alexander Blaess

(Original Key)

CLAUDE DEBUSSY

dole -
- gueur

V Up - - on _____ my ___
V Qui pé - nè -

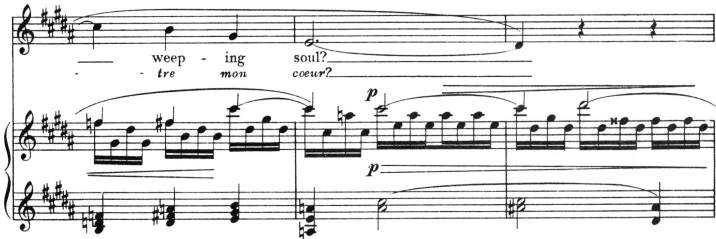

_____ weep - ing soul? _____
- tre mon coeur? _____

Oh! the soft sound of ___ rain, ___
O bruit doux de la ___ plui -

sempre pianissimo

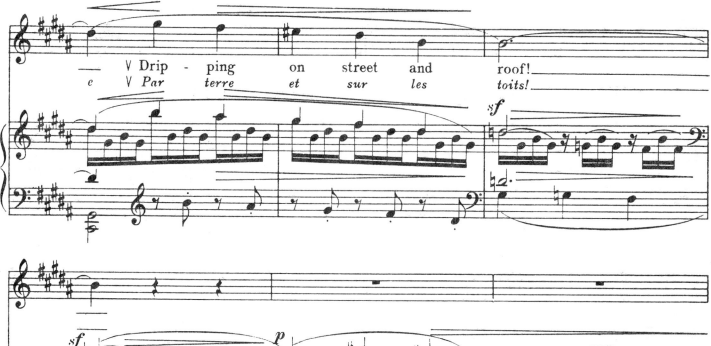

Drip - ping on street and roof!
e *Par terre* *et* *sur* *les* *toits!*

When my heart is in pain,
Pour *un* *coeur* *qui* *s'en* - *nui* - *e*

oh, the song of the
O *le* *chant* *de* *la*

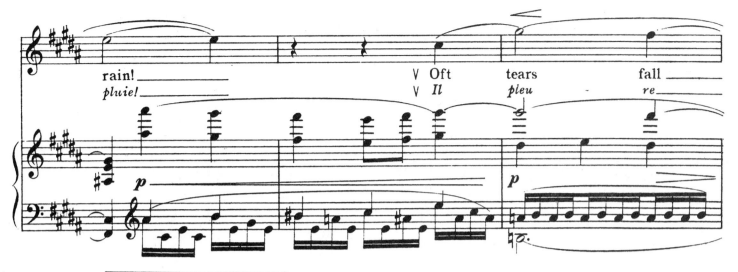

rain! _____
pluie! _____
Oft tears fall _____
Il pleu - re _____

with - out cause
sans rai - son
In my
Dans ce

soul
coeur
sick with sor -
qui se coeu -

- row.
- re.
Yet! _____
Quoi! _____
no sus - pi - cion
nul - le tra - hi

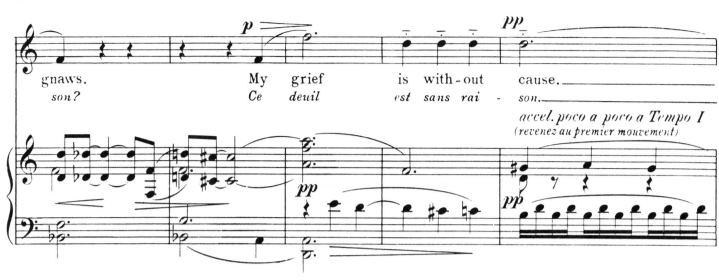

gnaws.
son?

My grief is with-out cause.
Ce deuil est sans rai - son.

accel. poco a poco a Tempo I
(revenez au premier mouvement)

Tempo I

I muse in bit - ter pain, V Ask - ing
C'est bien la pi - re pei - ne V De ne

won - d'ring - ly why, V free from love and hate's
sa - voir pour - quoi, V sans a - mour et sans

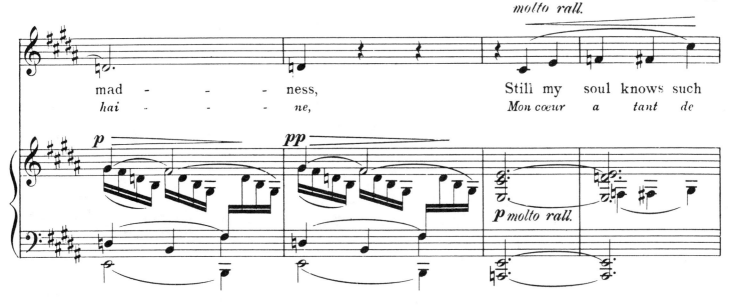

madness,
hai - - - ne,

Still my soul knows such
Mon cœur a tant de

sad - - - ness.
pei - - - ne!

EVENING HARMONY
(HARMONIE DU SOIR)
(Original Key, B)

CHARLES BAUDELAIRE
Translated by Isabella G. Parker

CLAUDE DEBUSSY

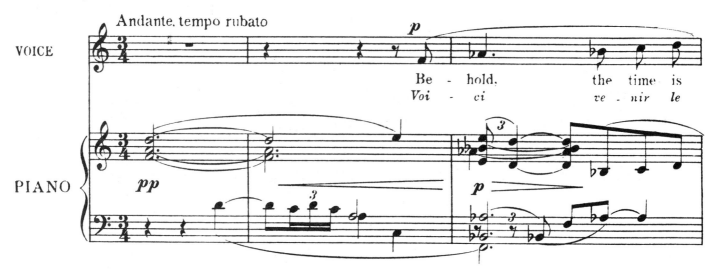

animando poco a poco

rare;
soir;

Trem-bles the vi - o - lin like a
Le vi - o - lon fré - mit comme un

heart that is break - ing.
coeur qu'on af - fli - ge;

poco string. poco cresc.

In the lan-guor - ous
Val - se mé - lan - co -

waltz its sad-ness is a - wak - ing.
lique et lan-gou - reux ver - ti - ge!

The
Le

sky   is   sad and   grand   like   a   great al-tar   there,
ciel   est   triste et   bĕau   comme   un   grand re - po   - soir.

Trem-bles the   vi - o - lin   like a   heart_____   that is break   - ing;
Le   vi - o - lon fré - mit   comme un   coeur_____   qu'on af - fli   - ge,

Heart most   ten - der   that   hates the   dark - ness   of   de -
Un   coeur   ten - dre,   qui   haït le   né - ant   vaste et

Bathed in blood is the sun, in its blood dark-ly flow-ing,
Le so-leil s'est noy-é dans son sang qui se fi-ge

Thy mem'-ry shines in my heart like cas-ket of gold.
Ton sou-ve-nir en moi luit comme un os-ten-soir!

molto rit.
(très retenu)

lento arpeggio
lentement arpégé

THE DEATH OF LOVERS
(LA MORT DES AMANTS)

CHARLES BAUDELAIRE
Translated by Isabella G. Parker

(Original Key)

CLAUDE DEBUSSY

Round our
Nous au -

beds shall sweet est o - dors be breath - ing, On couch - es so
rons des lits pleins d'o - deurs lé - gè - res, Des di - vans pro

deep calm - ly we shall lie,
fonds com - me des tom - beaux,

And ex - ot - ic flowers be o - ver us wreath - ing,
Et d'é - tran - ges fleurs sur des é - ta - gè - res,

molto dim.

Un - fold - ing for us 'neath a fair - er sky.
É - clo - ses pour nous sous des cieux plus beaux.

dim.

p

p

Em-ploy-ing at will all our life yet glow-ing, Our two hearts like blaz-ing
U - sant à l'en - vi. leurs cha - leurs d'er - niè - res, Nos deux cœurs se - ront deux

R.H.

p

p.

torch-es shall shine, Re - flect - ing the light we two are be - stow-ing
vas - tes flam - beaux, Qui ré - flé - chi - ront leurs dou - bles lu - miè - res

p.

On our spir - its twain like mir - rors di - vine.
Dans nos deux es - prits, ces mi - roirs ju - meaux.

ROMANCE

(Original Key)

PAUL BOURGET
Translated by Isabella G. Parker

CLAUDE DEBUSSY

Ah, whith-er is it borne a - way, This soul so di - vine of a
Ou donc les vents l'ont - ils chas - sée, Cette âme a - do - ra - ble des

flower? Is it the per-fume that re - main - eth,
lis? N'est - il plus un par - fum qui res - te

That heav'n-ly sweet-ness yet re - tain - eth Of days when thou my heart didst
De la su - a - vi - té cé - les - te Des jours ou tu m'en - ve - lop-

meno mosso (tempo rubato)

hold, As in ce - les - tial in - fluence ly - ing,
pais D'u - ne va - peur sur - na - tu - rel - - le

Tempo I

Of ro - sy hope, of love un - dy - ing, Of su - preme de -
Fai - te d'es-poir, d'amour fi - dè - le, De bé - a - ti -

Ritenuto

light, _____ peace un - told?
tude _____ et de paix?

THE SHADOW OF TREES
(L'OMBRE DES ARBRES)

(Original Key)

Le rossignol qui du haut d'une branche se regarde dedans, croit être tombé dans la rivière. Il est au sommet d'un chêne et toutefois il a peur de se noyer. (•

The nightingale, that, high up in the branches, sees his image reflected, believes he has fallen into the river. He is at the top of an oak, yet fears lest he should drown. (•

PAUL VERLAINE
Translated by Isabella G. Parker

CLAUDE DEBUSSY

(• Cyrano de Bergerac

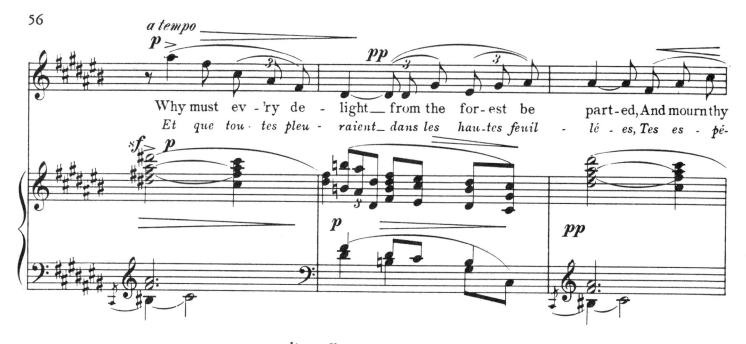

Why must ev-'ry de - light__ from the for-est be part-ed, And mourn thy
Et que tou-tes pleu - raient__ dans les hau-tes feuil - lé - es, Tes es - pé-

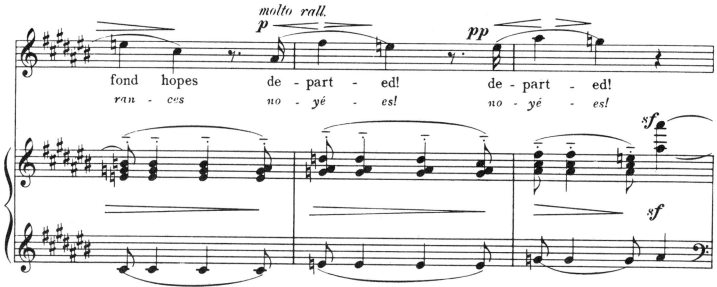

fond hopes de - part - ed! de - part - ed!
ran - ces no - yé - es! no - yé - es!

THE MAIDS OF CADIZ
(LES FILLES DE CADIX)

ALFRED DE MUSSET
Translated by Arthur Westbrook

LÉO DELIBES

ing; _____ The sky was blue, the breeze did blow, _____
tes, _____ Sur la pe - louse il fai - sait beau, _____

rall. *a tempo*

___ We danced the joy-ous bo - le - ro, _____ In mirth our hearts de - light -
___ Et nous dan-sions un bo - lé - ro _____ Au son des ca - sta - gnet -

colla voce   *a tempo*

rall.   **p** *un poco rit.*

- - - - ing. Neigh-bor, tell me pray,
tes: Dî - tes moi, voi - sin,

rall.   *sostenuto*

If my face is fair, Does this dress I wear Be - come me well to - day?
Si j'ai bon - ne mine, Et si ma bas - qui - ne Va bien ce ma - tin.

My waist you say is lithe and slen - der?
Vous me trou-vez la tail - le fi - ne?
My waist you say is lithe and trim,___
vous me trou-vez la tail - le fi -

ah! ah!___ ah! ah!___ ah!
-ne? ah! ah!___ ah! ah!___ ah!

___ We maid-ens of Ca - diz like well to hear such words,___ ah!___
___ *Les fil - les de Ca - dix ai-ment as-sez ce - la,*___ *ah!*___

ah!___ ah! ah! ah!___
*ah!*___ *ah!* *ah!* *ah!*___

poco rall.   _a tempo_

—We maid-ens of Ca - diz like well to hear such words, la ra la la la la
— _les fil - les de Ca - dix ai - ment as - sez ce - la,_ _la ra la la la la_

cresc.

la la ra la la la la la, We maid-ens of Ca - diz like well to hear such
la la ra la la la la la, les fil - les de Ca - dix ai - ment as - sez ce -

words.   ah! _____   ah! _____
_la._   _ah!_ _____   _ah!_ _____

p e staccato

cresc.

mf

But while we danced an - oth-er day _____
Et nous dan-sions un bo - lé - ro, _____

f *p*

_____ A bo-le - ro to - geth - - - - er, _____
_____ *Un soir, c'é-tait di - man - - - - che.* _____

_____ There came a cav - a - lier that way, _____
Vers nous s'en vient un hi - dal - go, _____

With lace of gold his cloak was gay, ____ And in his hat a
Cou - su d'or, la plume au cha - peau, ____ *Et le poing sur la*

colla voce *a tempo*

feath - - - - - er.
han - - - - - che:

If thou wilt be mine, Love - ly dark - eyed maid - en, Soon with jew - els la - den
Si tu veux de moi, *Brune au doux sou - ri - re,* *Tu n'as qu'à le di - re.*

sostenuto

Shall thy fin - gers shine. Nay, go your way, O gal - lant suit - or,
Cet or est à toi. *Pas - sez vo - tre che - min, beau si - re,*

diz such words don't un-der-stand, la ra la la la la   la la ra la la la la
dix n'en-ten-dent pas ce-la,   la ra la la la la   la la ra la la la la

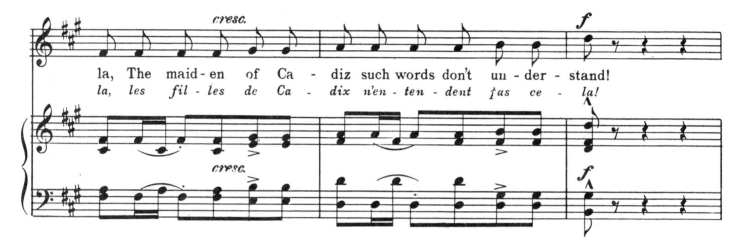

la, The maid-en of Ca - diz such words don't un - der - stand!
la, les fil - les de Ca - dix n'en - ten - dent pas ce - la!

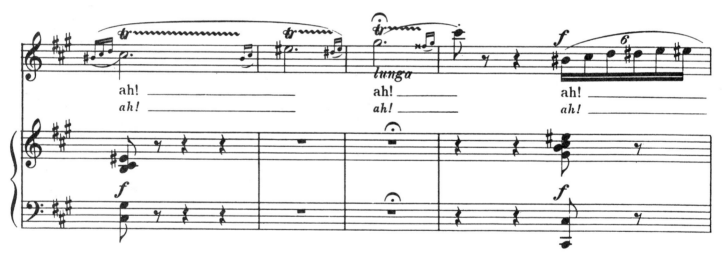

ah! _____   ah! _____   ah! _____
ah! _____   ah! _____   ah! _____

*BYGONE DAYS
(JOURS PASSÉS)

ARMAND SILVESTRE
Translated by Arthur Westbrook

LÉO DELIBES

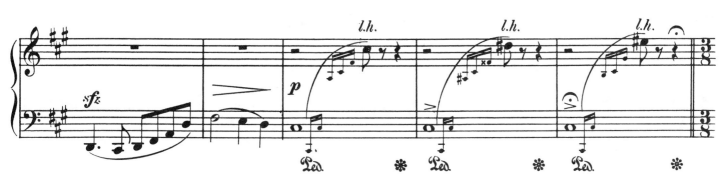

By - gone days! Oh!_____ how soon youth has fad - ed!
Jours pas - sés, O_____ jeu - nes - se en - vo - lé - e,

Still I mourn, Sor - row my soul has shad - ed.
Vous lais - sez L'á - me à ja - mais trou - blé - e.

*)The theme is from the ballet "La Source" by Delibes and Minkous (Opéra, Paris, 1866)

Oh! _____ how soon youth has fad -
O _____ jeu - nes - se en - vo - lé -

ed! Still I mourn, Sor - row has my spir - it o'er -
e, Vous lais - sez à _____ ja - mais mon â - me trou -

shad - ed. Bliss - ful spring! __ gone for aye! Oh, fra - grance of
blé - e. Ô prin - temps __ sans re - tour! Ô fleurs! ô dé -

flow - ers, __ of sweet flow-ers! Thy smile e'er brought me joy __ In those
li - re, __ ô dé - li - re, Quand mes yeux - cha que jour __ Te voy -

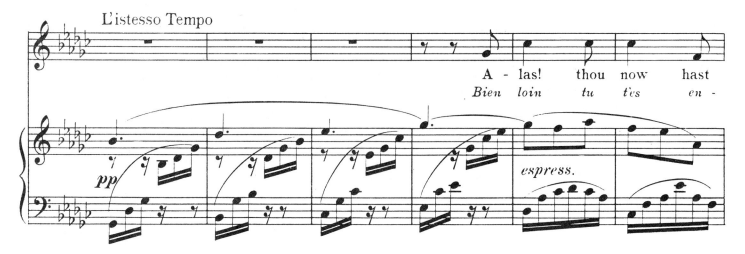

L'istesso Tempo

A - las! thou now hast
Bien loin tu t'es en -

left me, Of life it self be -
fui - e, Ô toi qui fus ma

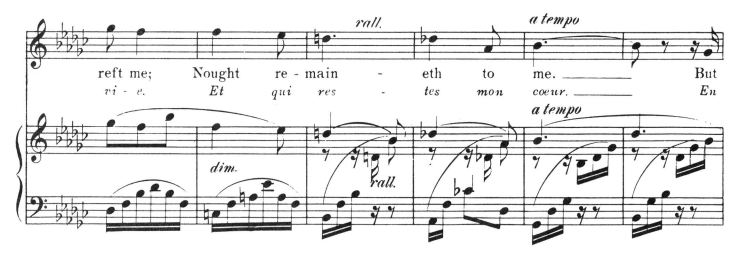

reft me; Nought re - main - eth to me. _____ But
vi - e. Et qui res - tes mon cœur. _____ En

vain _____ is Time's _____ en - deav - or, For my
vain _____ le temps _____ dé - vo - - re, Sous mon

heart hold-eth ev - er Mem - o-ries fond of
front luit en - co - - re Ton sou-ve - nir vain -

thee, Ah, mem'ries fond___ of thee! By - gone days,
queur, ton sou-ve - nir ___ vain-queur! Jours pas - sés.

Oh! _____ how soon youth has fad - ed, Still I mourn, Sor -
Ó _____ jeu - nes-se en vo - lé - e, Vous lais - sez à ___

- row has my spir-it o'er-shad - ed, By - gone days,___ by - gone
___ ja - mais mon â - me trou-blé - e, Jours pas - sés___ jours pas -

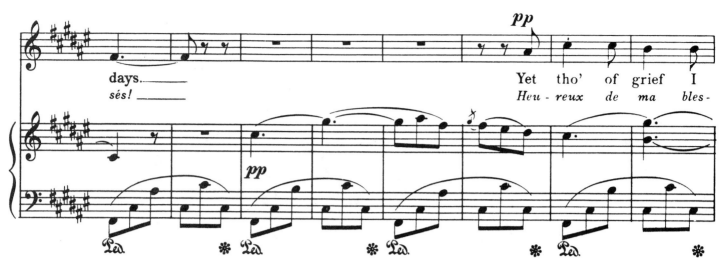

days._____ Yet tho' of grief I
sés! _____ Heu - reux de ma bles-

per-ish,_____ Thy name,_____ thy name I e'er will cher -
su - re, _____ Ton nom, _____ ton nom, je le mur - mu -

ish, And thou, who wert my be - ing, Ev - er liv - est in my___
re, O toi, qui fus ma vi - e Et__ qui res - - tes mon__

heart! _____
coeur! _____

à Monsieur Camille Benoit

ECSTASY
(EXTASE)

JEAN LAHOR
Translated by Isabella G. Parker

(Original Key)

HENRI DUPARC

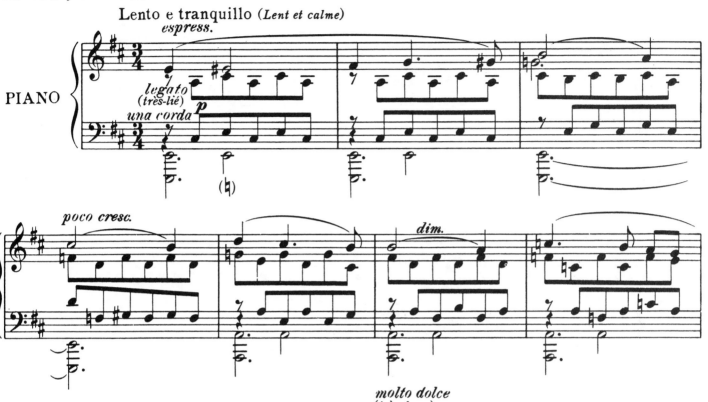

Copyright MCMIV by Oliver Ditson Company

On thy pale bos - om
Sur ton sein pâ - le

is my rest, And my slum - ber like death is
mon coeur dort D'un som-meil doux com - me la

blest._____
mort._____

à ma mère

A SIGH
(SOUPIR)

(Original Key)

A. SULLY-PRUDHOMME
Translated by Isabella G. Parker

HENRI DUPARC

Never more to see her or hear her,
Ne ja - mais la voir ni l'en - ten dre,

Never more to speak her dear name, Faith - ful
Ne ja - mais tout haut la nom - mer, mais, fi -

Ah! since I must _____ for- ev- er lan - guish,
Ah! ne pou - voir _____ que les lui ten - dre,

Con - sumed by tears and vain re - gret, _____
Et dans les pleurs se con - su - mer, _____

Still my tears con - vey all my
Mais ces pleurs tou - jours les ré -

an-guish; I love her yet.
pan-dre, Tou - jours l'ai - mer.

à Mr Emmanuel Jadin

MOONLIGHT
(CLAIR DE LUNE)
(MENUET)

PAUL VERLAINE
Translated by Alexander Blaess

(Original Key, Bb minor)

GABRIEL FAURÉ

Andantino quasi Allegretto

Chant - ing the while strains of mi - nor mode, Tri - um-phant love___
Tout en chan - tant, sur le mo-de mi - neur, L'a - mour vain - queur___

___ and joy___ of life ex - toll - - ing,
___ et la___ vie op - por - tu - - ne,

They seem to doubt that love and joy are real, And in - to
Ils n'ont pas l'air de croire à leur bon - heur, Et leur chan-

moon-beams wan their song is wo - - ven;
son se mêle au clair de lu - - ne!

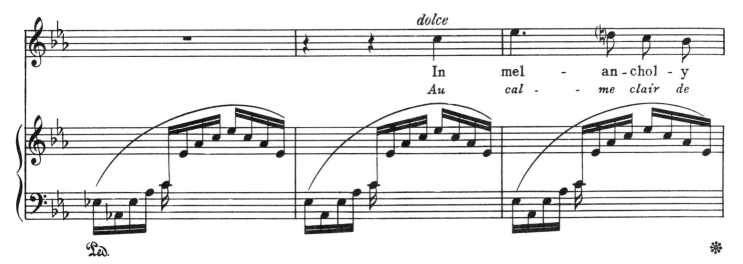

dolce

In mel - an-chol - y
Au cal - - me clair de

moon - light, sad and calm, That
lu - ne, tris - te et beau, *Qui*

dolce

brings the birds ten - der dreams in the
fait rê - ver les oi - seaux dans les

wil - - lows, Mak - ing. the foun-tains
ar - - bres, *Et san - glo - ter d'ex -*

sob with ec - sta - sy;
ta - - se les jets d'eau.

'Mong sta - tues___ cold, of white and pur - est___
Les grands jets d'eau svel - - tes par - mi___ les___

pp sempre

mar - - ble.
mar - - bres!

à Mlle. Alice Boissonnet

THE CRADLES
(LES BERCEAUX)
(MÉLODIE)
(Original Key, B♭ minor)

A. SULLY-PRUDHOMME
Translated by Isabella G. Parker

GABRIEL FAURÉ

The state-ly ships a-long the quay,
Le long du Quai, les grands vais-seaux,

Where the waves a-round them are play - - ing, The
Que la hou-le in-cli - ne en si - len - - ce, Ne

cra - dles for-get, si - - lent-ly,
pren - nent pas gar - - de aux ber-ceaux,

OSSIA

By the moth-er's hand gen-tly sway - ing. ____
Que la main des fem - mes ba - lan - ce. ____

cresc. poco a poco

But the day of part - ing will come,
Mais vien - dra le jour des a - dieux,

Moth - er's tears must be sad - ly flow - - ing,
Car il faut que les fem - mes pleu - - rent,

cresc. molto

When man will sail, ea - ger to roam,
Et que les hom - - mes cu - ri - eux

cresc. molto

Daunt - less to far ho - ri - zons go - - ing. _____
Ten - tent les ho - ri - zons qui leur - - rent! _____

Those state-ly ships__ up - on __ that day,
Et ce jour-là __ les grands__ vais-seaux,

While the re - ced - ing port is wan - - ing,
Fuy - ant le port qui di - mi - nu - - e,

Mys - te - rious-ly feel force de-tain - ing
Sen - tent leur mas - - se re - te - nu - e

From those souls cra - dled
Par l'â - me des loin -

far _____ a - way,
tains _____ ber - ceaux,

From those souls cra - dled
Par l'â - me des loin -

far ____ a - way. _____
tains ____ ber - ceaux. _____

à *Mademoiselle Louise Collinet*

THE ROSES OF ISPAHAN
(LES ROSES D'ISPAHAN)

(Original Key, D)

LECONTE DE LISLE
Translated by Alexander Blaess

GABRIEL FAURÉ

Have not as fresh a per-fume, nor so sweet a fra-grance, O fair-est
Ont un par-fum moins frais, ont u-ne o-deur moins dou-ce, Ô blan-che

Le-ï-lah! as thy zeph-yr-like breath.
Le-ï-lah! que ton souf-fle lé-ger.

As cor-al are thy
Ta lè-vre est de co-

lips, and thy sil-ver-y laugh Shames the spring as its rip-ples purl in song me-
rait et ton ri-re lé-ger___ son-ne mieux que l'eau vi-___ve et d'u-ne voix plus

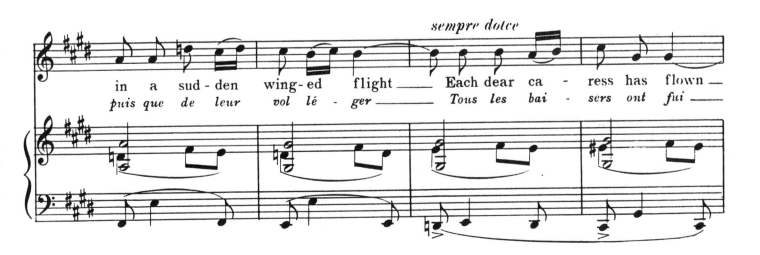

from thy lips hon-eyed sweet - ness, _____ All the per-fume has
_ de ta lè-vre si dou - ce _____ Il n'est plus de par-

waned from the pale or-ange-tree, Bar-ren are rose and jas-mine of their balmy
fum dans le pá-le o-ran-ger, Ni de cé-les-te a-rome aux ro-ses dans leur

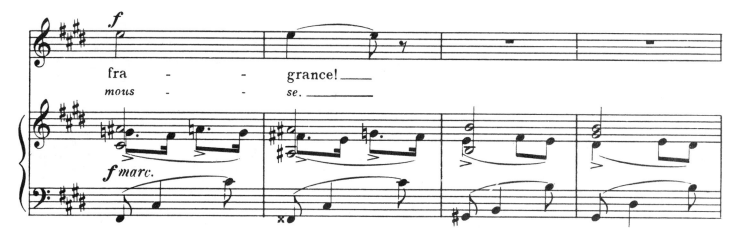

fra - - grance! _____
mous - - se. _____

Oh! let thy bud-ding love, that but-ter-fly So
Oh! que ton jeu-ne a - mour, ce pa-pil-lon lé-

frail, A - gain up - on my heart, a - light in do - cile bond - -

ger, Re - vien - ne vers mon coeur d'u - ne ai - le promp-te et dou - -

cresc. poco a poco

age. And thus re - store its per-fume to the or-ange tree,

ce. Et qu'il par - fu - me en - cor la fleur de l'o - ran ger

poco rit.   *a tempo*

f

To Is - pa - han's fair rose In its green moss en - fold -

Les ro - ses d'Is - pa - han dans leur gai - ne de mous -

mf   *p*

ed. ____

se. ____

a Madame Trélat

MARRIAGE OF ROSES
(LE MARIAGE DES ROSES)

(Original Key)

EUGÈNE DAVID

Translated by Isabella G. Parker

CÉSAR FRANCK

lov - ed, knows't thou how sweet, the mar-riage of ro - ses? V A

gnon - ne, sais - tu com - ment S'é - pou - sent les ro - ses? V Ah!

un - ion full and com - plete, _____ ∨ un - ion full and com -
cet hy - men est char - mant, _____ ∨ cet hy - men est char -

plete! ____ ∨ Ten - der speech dis - clos - es Lov - ing
munt! ____ ∨ Quel - les ten - dres cho - ses El - les

thought, as, soft - ly bright _____ ∨ Each fair eye - lid un -
di - sent en ou - vrant _____ ∨ Leurs pau - piè - res

poco rall.

clos - es! ∨ Be - lov - ed, knows't thou how sweet The mar - riage of
clo - ses! ∨ Mi - gnon - ne, sais - tu com - ment S'é - pou - sent les

poco rall.

ros - - ses? ∨ This they say; ∨ O let us love,—
ro - - ses? ∨ El - les di - sent: ∨ aim - ons nous!—

— ∨ So soon life is end - ing! ∨ Then with fon - der kiss of love —
— ∨ si courte est la vi - e! ∨ Ay - ons les bai - sers plus doux —

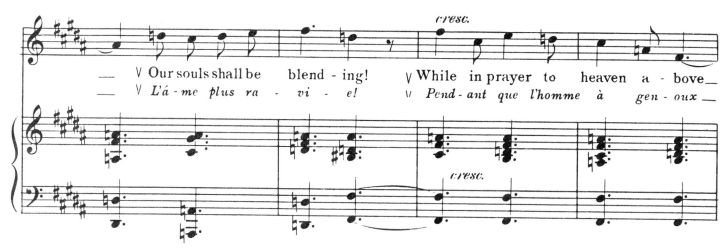

— ∨ Our souls shall be blend - ing! ∨ While in prayer to heaven a - bove—
— ∨ L'â - me plus ra - vi - e! ∨ Pend - ant que l'homme à gen - oux —

— ∨ With hope man is bend ing: ∨ Sis - ters, let us on - ly love!
— ∨ Doute, es - père ou pri - e! ∨ Ó mes sœurs, em - bras - sons - nous!

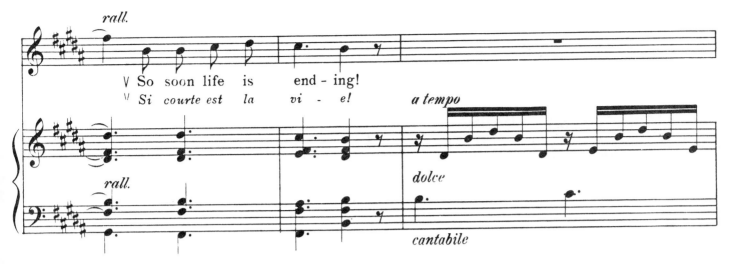

thee, _____ ⱽ Spring-time com - eth to thee _____
toi, _____ ⱽ Le prin - temps vient à toi _____

And the swal - lows, tell - ingⱽHow love reigns a - lone and
Et des hi - ron - del - les ⱽAi - mer est l'u - ni - que

cresc.

free _____ In their faith - ful dwell - ing. ⱽ Oh, my
loi _____ A leurs nids _____ fi - dè - les. ⱽ O ma

cresc.

poco rit.

Queen, ___ fol - low thy King. ⱽ Such love must we cher - ish,
rei - ne, ˒ suis ton roi, ⱽ Ai - mons-nous comme el - les.

poco rit.

à mon ami Albert Cahen (d'Anvers)

THE GATHERED ROSE
(LIED)

LUCIEN PATÉ
Translated by Isabella G. Parker

(Original Key)

CÉSAR FRANCK

gen - tle hand for me did sev - er Rose - bud so fair, As
moi sa main cueil - lait des ro - ses À ce buis - son, Comme

pure and ten - der as the giv - er, Blos - som most rare. The
elle en - core à peine è - clo - ses, Chè - re mois - son. La

flower, a - las! too ear - ly__ dy - ing,- She was so dear! The
gerbe, hé - las! en est fa - né - e Comme elle aus - si; La

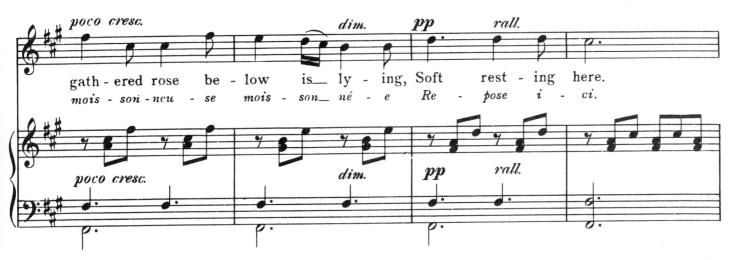

gath - ered rose be - low is ly__ ing, Soft rest - ing here.
mois - son - neu - se mois - son né - e Re - pose i - ci.

But o'er the tomb where
Mais sur la tom - be

now re - pos - eth Love, for a - while, An
qui vous cou - vre, O mes a - mours! Une

eg - lan -tine but half un-clos-eth, Bright with a smile. And
é - glan - ti - ne, qui s'entr'ou - vre, Sou - rit tou - jours. Et

'neath the bush that o'er her bend -eth, Where we were
sous le buis - son qui sur-plom - be, Quand je re -

met. Her voice to me this mes - sage send - eth:—
viens, U - ne voix me dit sous la tom - be:—

"I'll not for - get."
"Je me sou - viens."

REMEMBRANCE
(TE SOUVIENS-TU?)

BENJAMIN GODARD
Translated by Alexander Blaess

BENJAMIN GODARD

Dost thou re-call thy wist-ful prom - ise,
Te sou - viens - tu de ta pro - mes - se?

Dost thou re-call the hap-py past?
Te sou - viens - tu des ans pas - sés?

Dost thou re-call our thrill-ing rap - ture?
Te sou - viens - tu de no-tre i - vres - se

When in my arms I held thee fast?____
*Quand nos bras é-taient en-la-cés?*____

Oh, guard me well thy heart's af-
Oh! gar-de-moi bien ta ten-

fec-tion; In bit-ter want I need thy kiss!____
*dres - se, J'ai tant be-soin de tes bai-sers!*____

Dost thou re-call my tear-ful sad - ness,
Te sou-viens-tu de ma tris-tes - se

When for one day we had to part?
Lors - que je par-tais pour un jour?

COME AND EMBARK!
(EMBARQUEZ-VOUS!)

ULRICH GUTTINGUER
Translated by Charles Fonteyn Manney

(Original Key)

BENJAMIN GODARD

god of these wa-ters is Cu - pid; Be - ware lest he choose_ a
dieu de ces ri-ants ri-va - ges, Le tendre_ A - mour_ veil -

fa - tal mark. Young_ and old,_ fool-ish and wise,_
le sur nous. Jeu - nes et vieux,_ fol - les et sa - ges,_

Come all! em-bark! Far from the
Em - bar - quez-vous! Je vais du

shore now we are drift-ing; O'er the riv-er our boat shall dart; Li-sa
pied, loin de le ri - ve Pous-ser le ba-teau va-cil - lant Li - se,

dear, no lon-ger be fear-ful; Hold me close to thy trem-bling____
ne sois pas si crain-ti - ve, Pres - se moi sur ton coeur trem -

heart.____ Ah, how can'st thou fear an-y dan - ger? To
blant.____ Eh! quoi, tu crain-drais les nau-fra - ges! Pé -

per-ish to-geth-er would bliss af-ford!   Young and old,
rir en-sem-ble se - rait doux   Jeu - nes et vieux,

fool-ish and wise,   Come all! on board!
fol - les et sa - ges,   Em - bar - quez - vous!

To that fair isle I fain would con-
Je veux vous con-dui - re moi-

duct thee,   Where they dance to a joy-ous song;   Where of thy
mê - me   Dans l'île où l'on danse aux chan - sons;   Où de la

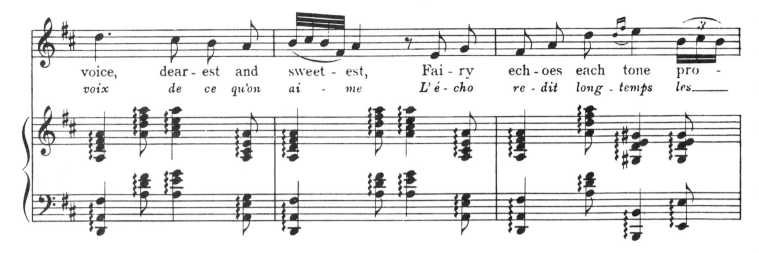

voice, dear-est and sweet-est, Fai-ry ech-oes each tone pro-
*voix de ce qu'on ai - me L'é - cho re - dit long - temps les*___

long.___ Bright pleas-ure de-lights e'er to wan - der, Come
sons.___ Le plai - sir ai - me les voy - a - ges, A-

friends, come com-rades ere night grows dark. Young___ and old,___
mis,___ pa - rents,___ ac - cou - rez tous. Jeu - nes et vieux;___

fool - ish and wise,_____ Come all! em - bark!
fol - les et sa - ges;_____ Em - bar - quez - vous!

LOVE
(L'AMOUR)

ROSE HAREL
Translated by Arthur Westbrook

BENJAMIN GODARD

love ____ thee as a hope a - ris - ing, ____ New-ly born,
t'ai - me, com - me l'es - pé - ran - ce Qui re - naît

from the blackest sky. I love thee as the peace - ful si - lence,
sous l'ho - ri - zon noir, Je t'ai - me, com - me le si - len - ce

Through ____ which eve - ning's
Que ____ frois - se la

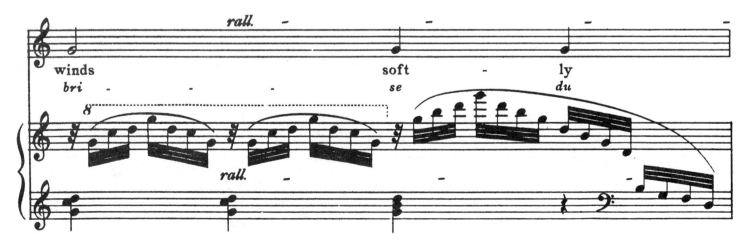

winds soft - ly
bri - se du

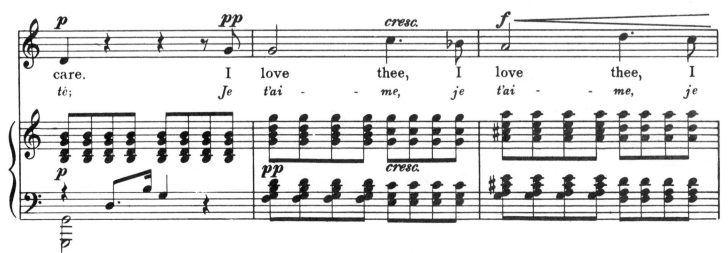

love _____ thee, e'en as my soul de-vot - ed Lov-ing-ly longs
t'ai - me en-fin com-me mon â - me Ai - me d'am-our

for heav'n a-bove; As doth an an-gel fair and ho - ly Ev - er-
le beau ciel bleu, Com - me le ché-ru-bin en flam - - me À ja-

more his Cre - a - tor love.
mais ai - me - ra son Dieu!

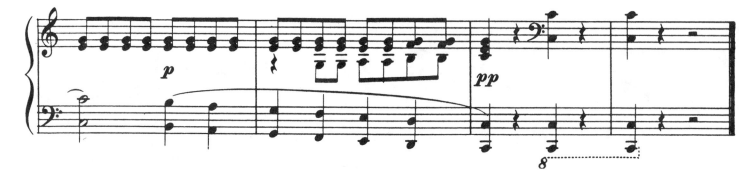

To Mme. Conneau
TO SPRING
(AU PRINTEMPS)

JULES BARBIER
Translated by Charles Fonteyn Manney

CHARLES GOUNOD

Win - ter yields to the wiles of spring,
Le prin - temps chas - se les hi - vers

In the for - est the bird - lings sing,
Et sou - rit dans les ar - bres verts

Ver - dant mead - ows are gay___ a - new___ with
Sous la feuil - le nou - vel - le pas - sent

bud and blos - som.
des bruits d'ai - le!

Let us roam in the sha - dy grove,
Viens, sui - vons les sen - tiers om - breux,

Breath - ing vows___ of deep - est love.
Où s'é - ga - rent les a - mou - reux,

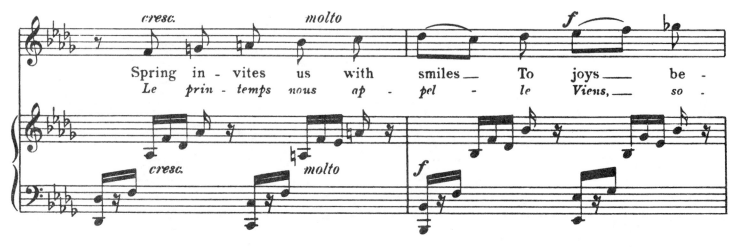

Spring in - vites us with smiles___ To joys___ be -
Le prin - temps nous ap - pel - le Viens,___ so -

yond   com - pare.____
yons   heu - reux.____

dim.

incalzando
(chaud et contenu)
p

Bright - ly   the   sun - beams   are   glanc - ing,
Vois!   le   so - leil   é - tin - cel - le,

p

cresc.   *un poco rit.*   *a tempo*

In   thy   dear   eyes   bright - er   danc - ing,
Et   sa   clar - té   qui   ruis - sel - le,

colla voce   *a tempo*

f

Mak - ing   still   more   en - tranc - ing____   Thy
Me   sem - ble en - cor   plus   bel - le ____   Dans

beau - ty rare.
tes beaux yeux!

Let us roam in the sha - dy grove,
Viens, sui - vrons les sen - tiers om - breux,

Breath - ing vows___ of deep - est love.
Où s'é - ga - rent les a - mou - reux,

Spring in - vites us with smiles___ To joys___ be -
Le prin - temps nous ap - pel - le, Viens,___ so -

yond com - pare._____ Let thy sweet voice, up - ward

yons heu - reux!_____ Que ta voix chante et se

soar - ing, Join with the lark's out - pour - ing,

mê - le A l'har - mo - nie é - ter - nel - le,

Rais - ing a song a - dor - ing__ Thro' skies so

Je crois en - ten - dre en el - le__ chan - ter les

fair._____ Let us roam in the shad - y grove,

cieux!_____ Viens sui - vons les sen - tiers om - breux,

Breath-ing vows— of deep - est love. Spring in-vites us with
Où së - ga - rent les a - mou - reux. *Le prin- temps nous ap -*

smiles To joys— be - yond com - pare.————
pel - le. Viens, so - yons heu - reux!————

À Madame Jules Barbier

MEDJÉ
(AN ARABIAN SONG)
(CHANSON ARABE)

JULES BARBIER
Translated by Arthur Westbrook

CHARLES GOUNOD

Allegretto (molto moderato)

O Med-jé, en - chain'd I'm yield - ing,
Ô Med-jé, qui d'un sou - ri - re

To thy smile a will-ing slave; As em - press thy scep-tre wield - ing, My
En-chai-nas ma li-ber - té. Sois fiè - re de ton em - pi - re Com-

free - dom to thee I gave. No more my glad way pur - su - ing, Like
mande à ma vo-lon - té. Na - guère en-cor, sans en - tra - ves, Com-

*Pronounce, "Mĕd-yea"

some wild bird of the sea,___ I must heed thy glance sub-du-ing, Who
me l'oi-seau dans les airs,___ Ton re - gard a fait es-cla-ve Le

roam'd the wide des-ert free.___ Med - jé!___ Med - jé!___ The
libre en-fant des dé - serts.___ Med - jé!___ Med - jé!___ La

voice___ of love's e - mo-tion Should thy___ com-pas-sion move!___ A -
voix___ de l'a-mour mê - me De - vrait___ te dés-ar - mer!___ Hé -

las! _____ Why doubt my heart's de - vo-tion, When I die for thy
las! _____ Tu dou-tes que je l'ai - me Quand je meurs de t'ai-

love! _____ When I die for thy love! _
mer! _____ *Quands je meurs de t'ai - mer!* _

These rich gems, _____ thy charms en-hanc - ing, All with en - vy may be -
Ces bi - joux _____ que l'on t'en-vi e J'ai ven-du pour les pa -

hold; _____ To pay for their bril-liant glanc - ing My
yer. _____ In - gra - te plus que ma vi - e, Mes

arms and my steed I sold!___ The spell is ev - er___
ar - mes et mon cour - sier! ___ Et tu de - man - des quels

cresc.

grow - ing, Which to thy side binds me fast.___ Dost not
char - mes Tien - nent mon coeur en - i - vré?___ Tu n'as

dim.

p

see my tears still flow - ing? Wilt thou not yield thee at
donc pas vu mes lar - mes? Tou - te la nuit j'ai pleu -

cresc.

dim.

p

last?___ Med - jé! ___ Med - jé! ___ The
ré! ___ Med - jé! ___ Med - jé! ___ Les

p

tears ___ of love's e - mo - tion   Should   thy ___ com-pas-sion
pleurs ___ de l'a-mour   mê - me   De - vraient ___ te dés-ar-

move! ___   A - las! _____   Dost doubt my heart's de -
mer! ___   Hé - las! _____   tu dou-tes que je

vo - tion,   When I die   for thy   love! _____
t'ai - me   Quand je meurs   de t'ai - mer! _____

When I die   for thy   love! ___
Quand je meurs de t'ai - mer! ___

If my heart___ thou wouldst be read - ing, Plunge this dag-ger in my
Tu veux li - re dans mon â - me pour y voir ton nom vain-

breast!___ And while for thee it is bleed - ing, Thy
queur!___ Eh bien! prends donc cet - te la - me Et

name thou'lt find there im - press'd.___ Be - hold, then, in bright - ness
plon - ge la dans mon coeur!___ Re - gar - de sans é - pou-

shin - ing, Thy soul un-moved as of yore,___ Thine own
van - te Et sans re - grets su - per - flus___ Ton i -

im - age fair, en - twin - ing With the heart___ that beats no
mage en - cor vi - van - te Dans ce coeur___ qui ne bat

more!___ Med - jé!___ Med - jé!___ My
plus!___ Med - jé!___ Med - jé!___ Le

blood,___ my last e - mo - tion Should thy___ com-pas-sion
sang___ de l'a-mour mê - me De - vrait___ te dés - ar -

THE VALLEY
(LE VALLON)

ALPHONSE de LAMARTINE
Translated by Arthur Westbrook

CHARLES GOUNOD

My heart doth long for rest, hope in my breast has
Mon coeur las-sé de tout, mê - me de l'es-pé-

fad - ed; And no more do I crave___ joys which the fates de - ny! In the
ran - ce, N'i-ra plus de ses voeux___ im - por - tu - ner le sort! Prê-tez

home of my youth,___ the vale___ so green and shad - ed, Let an
- moi seu - le - ment,___ val - lon___ de mon en - fan - ce, Un a -

hour of re - pose___ bring me peace ere I
- si - le d'un jour___ pour at - ten - dre la

die.___
mort!___

My life___ seems like a
Di - ci___ je vois la

vi - sion. from the past now for - sa - ken,
vi - e à tra - vers un nu - a - ge

Shad - ow'd with heav - y clouds,___ Il - lumed___ by no bright ray;___
S'é - va - nou - ir pour moi___ dans___ l'om - bre du pas - sé!___

Love a - lone still re - mains,___ as when from sleep we wa - ken There sur -
L'a - mour seul est res - té___ comme u - ne grande i - ma - ge Sur - vit

cre - scen - - do -

vives one clear im - age from dreams pass'd a - way.___
seule au ré - veil dans un songe ef - fa - cé!___

poco rit.

f   dim. - - - - p

a tempo

Rest thou, my soul, be pa - tient; here lies thy goal be -
Re - po - se - toi, mon â - me, en ce der - nier a -

fore thee, And like_____ a Pil-grim worn,_____ yet with
si - le Ain - si_____ qu'un voy - a - geur_____ qui, le

heart free__ from care, Pause at the o - pen gate, while
cœur plein__ d'es - poir S'as - sied a - vant d'en - trer, aux

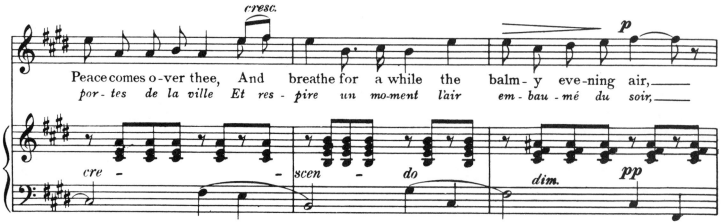

Peace comes o - ver thee, And breathe for a while the balm - y eve-ning air,_____
por - tes de la ville Et res - pire un mo - ment l'air em - bau - mé du soir,_____

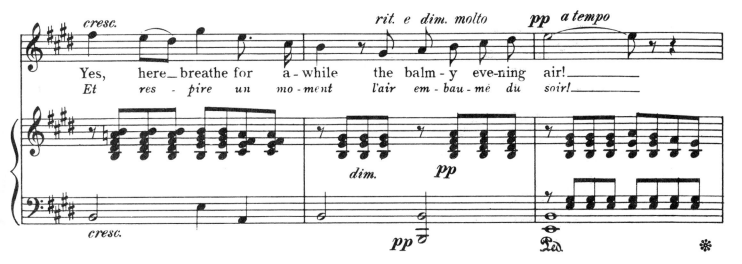

Yes, here breathe for a-while the balm-y eve-ning air!
Et res - pire un mo - ment l'air em - bau - mé du soir!

Thy
Tes

days draw to a close sad au-tumn winds are
jours tris - tes et courts com - me des jours d'au -

sigh - ing, While shades of com - ing night wrap the world in
tom - ne Dé - cli - nent com - me l'ombre au pen - chant des cô -

breast _____ find re - pose, Tho' the world should grow cold, all thy
t'ou - - vre tou - jours Quand tout chan - ge pour toi la na -

wounds she can heal, And the life - giv - ing sun in change-less splen-dor glows, ___
ture est la même Et le mê - me so - leil se lè - ve sur tes jours! ___

Yes, the ___ life - giv - ing sun in change-less splen-dor glows! ___
Oui, le ___ mê - me so - leil se lè - ve sur tes jours! ___

THE PERFECT HOUR
(L'HEURE EXQUISE)

PAUL VERLAINE
Translated by Alexander Blaess

(Original Key, B)

REYNALDO HAHN

COULD MY SONGS THEIR WAY BE WINGING
(SI MES VERS AVAIENT DES AILES!)

VICTOR HUGO
Translated by Charles Fonteyn Manney

REYNALDO HAHN

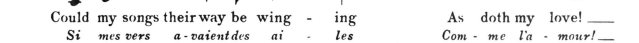

à Madame Brunet-Lafleur

MADRIGAL
(MADRIGAL)
DANS LE STYLE ANCIEN
(In the old manner)

ROBERT de BONNIÈRES
Translated by Isabella G. Parker

VINCENT D'INDY

(Original Key)

Where can you find more charm-ing face or fair - er,
Qui ja - mais fut de plus char-mant vi - sa - ge,

A snow-ier neck, where soft hair silk - en lies?__ Where was thére
De col plus blanc, de che - veux plus soy - eux;__ Qui ja - mais

ev - er form of beau - ty rar - er Than hath my la - dy of
fut de plus gen - til cor - sa - ge. Qui ja - mais fut que ma

love - li - est eyes?
Dame aux doux yeux!

a tempo

Where can you find lips ___ more sweet, ev - er smil - ing, Un - to whose
Qui ja - mais eut lè - - vres plus sou - ri - an - tes, Qui sou - ri -

a tempo

smil - ing the fond heart re - plies, ___ Or breast more chaste, 'neath
ant ren - dit coeur plus joy - eux, Plus cha - ste sein sous

veil of gauze be-guil-ing, Than hath my la-dy of love-li-est
guim-pes trans-pa-ren-tes, Qui ja-mais eut que ma Dame aux doux

eyes! Where is a voice of
yeux! Qui ja-mais eut voix

mu-sic more en-tranc-ing, Or teeth whose white-ness
d'un plus doux en-ten-dre, Mi-gnon-nes dents qui

à X

A SEA SONG
(LIED MARITIME)

(Original Key)

VINCENT D'INDY
Translated by Isabella G. Parker

VINCENT D'INDY

Lento moderato (♩=76)
(Modérémént lent)

VOICE

PIANO

A - far in the o - cean sink - eth the sun, ___
Au loin, dans la mer, s'é - teint le so - leil,___

___ And the sea is tran - quil and tide - less; The
___ *et la mer est calme et sans ri - de;* *le*

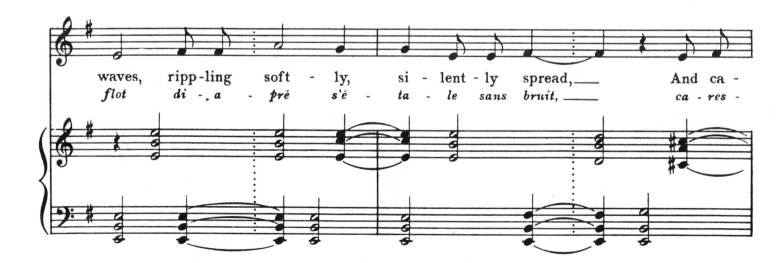

waves, ripp - ling soft - ly, si - lent - ly spread, ___ And ca -
flot di - a - pré s'é - ta - le sans bruit, ___ *ca - res -*

ress the strand — as it dark - ens; Thine
sant la grève — *as - som - bri - e;* *Tes*

eyes,   thy faith - less eyes are closed, — And my
yeux, *tes traî - tres yeux sont clos, —* *et mon*

heart is at rest, is calm   like the
cœur est tran - quil - - le com - - - me la

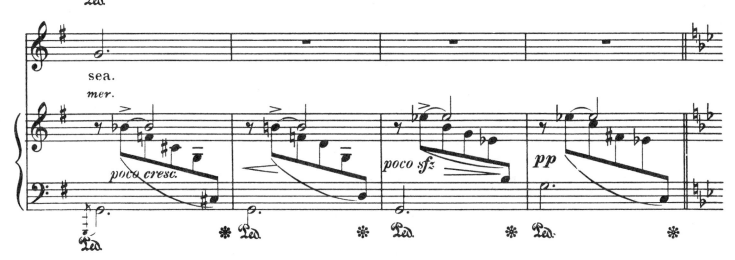

sea.
mer.

Più animato (♩ :112)
(Plus animé)

far   on the sea   the
loin,   *sur la mer,*   *l'o -*

storm   com - eth   on, _____   And the
rage   est le - vé. _____   *et la*

Ped.

o - - cean wild - - ly is
mer s'e - meut et bouil -

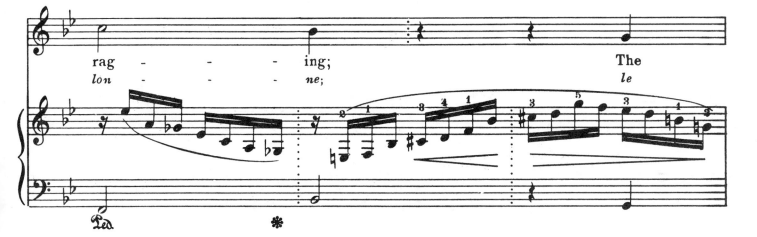

rag - - - ing; The
lon - - ne; le

Ped. ✻

waves to the skies mount
flot, jus - qu'aux cieux, s'e - -

poco più f

proud - ly a - loft, _____ Then
ri - ge su - perbe, _____ et

heart   in its   pain, ___   my heart   in its   joy,   With
coeur   tor-tu - ré, ___   mon   coeur   bien-heu - reux   s'ex -

rall.
(en retenant)

rap -   ture   as -   cends,   then   breaks
alte   *et*   *se*   *bri -*   *- se*   *com -*

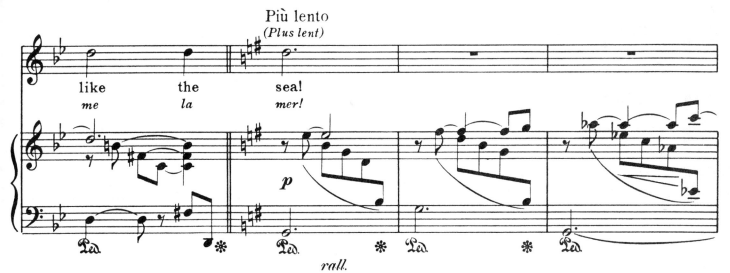

Più lento
(Plus lent)

like   the   sea!
me   *la*   *mer!*

rall.
(en ralentissant)

PROVENCE SONG
(CHANT PROVENÇAL)

MICHEL CARRÉ
Translated by Isabella G. Parker

JULES MASSENET

Andantino sostenuto

Mi - rel - la doth not know she hold - eth Such a charm___ in her win-some grace!
Mi - reil - le ne sait pas en - co - re Le doux char - me de sa beau - té!

She like a love - ly bud un - fold - eth When smiled up - on by sum - mer's face!
C'est u - ne fleur qui vient dé - clo - re Dans un sou - ri - re de l'é - té!

Who know-eth not Mi - rel - la, los - eth Heav'n's
À qui ne con - naît pas Mi - reil - le, Dieu

choic-est gift of treas -ure rare!_____ Her beau -ty a ri -val re-
ca -che son plus cher__ tré -sor!_____ Sa grâ -ce à nulle au -tre pa-

fus -eth With gold -en dress__ be-yond com -pare!
reil -le La pa -re mieux__ qu'un man -teau d'or!

Mi -rel -la doth not know she hold -eth Such a charm____ in her win-some
Mi -reil -le ne sait pas en -co -re Le doux char -me de sa beau-

grace!
té!

She like a love -ly bud un-
C'est u -ne fleur qui vient d'é-

OPEN THY BLUE EYES
(OUVRE TES YEUX BLEUS)

154

PAUL ROBIQUET
Translated by Arthur Westbrook

(Original Key, F)

JULES MASSENET

Allegro, con molto anima
(Avec assez d'animation)

He *(Lui)*

O - pen thy blue eyes now, my dar - - - ling, 'Tis dawn of day;
Ou - vre tes yeux bleus, ma mi - gnon - - - ne: Voi - ci le jour.

On the leaf - y bough trills the star - - ling His am'-rous lay.
Dé - jà la fau - vet - te fre - don - - ne Un chant d'a - mour.

Au - ro - ra with the hue of ro - - ses
L'au - rore é - pa - nou - it la ro - se.

Doth tinge the skies; The
Viens a - vec moi *Cueil -*

love - - ly mar - gue - rite un - clos - - - es;
lir la mar - gue -.rite é - clo - - - se.

My love, a - rise!
Ré - veil - - le - toi!

My love, a - rise!
Ré - veil - le - toi!

HOW BRIEF IS THE HOUR
(QUE L'HEURE EST DONC BRÈVE)

ARMAND SILVESTRE
Translated by Isabella G. Parker

JULES MASSENET

SERENADE
(SÉRÉNADE)

(Original Key, D)

EUGÈNE ADENIS
Translated by Isabella G. Parker

GABRIEL PIERNÉ

Up - on the breast of_ night_____ A star is gleam-ing bright._
Au sein des nuits tout dort,_____ L'é-toi - le brille en - cor,_

The wind is soft be - low,_____ Where li-lacs blow;_____
Le vent se tait là - bas,_____ Dans les li - las._____

Be-neath the fo -liage blest_____ The bird has
Sous le feuil-lage a - mi,_____ L'oi-seau s'est

gone to_ rest.___ Come, the for-est gloom Sheds rich per-fume; Up-on the
en - dor - mi.___ Viens, les bois char - més Sont em-bau - més; Au sein des

breast of_ night,___ Yes, A star is gleam-ing bright. Come, O thou my
nuits tout_ dort.___ Oui, l'é - toi-le brille en - cor, Viens, ô mon a -

love, for I am thine. Be on - ly mine! Let our sweet musings
mour, je t'ap-par - tiens, Sois toute à moi!___ Lais - sons er - rer nos

wan - der Through paths of per-fume and of song.___
â - mes Sur les par - fums et les chan - sons.___

Let our love___ to dreams be long.___
Ai - mons - nous,___ ai - mons, rê - vons.___

But a - las!___ are my la - bors in vain?___
Mais hé - las!___ est-ce en vain que ma voix___

No ech - o___ re - sponds___ yet a - gain.
Fait gé - mir___ l'é - cho___ de ces bois?

Come, soft is the air. Night is so fair, Ah! come!___ Ah! come!___
Viens, l'air est si doux Au - tour de nous, Ah! viens!___ Ah! viens!___

The bird hath gone to rest. Come, the for-est
L'oi - seau s'est en - dor - mi. *Viens, les bois char -*

gloom Sheds rich per - fume; Up - on the breast of night,
més Sont em - bau - més; Au sein des nuits tout dort.

Yes, A star is gleam-ing bright. Come, O thou my
Oui, l'é - toi - lé brille en - cor, Viens, ô mon a -

love, For I am thine. Be on - ly mine!
mour, je t'ap - par - tiens, Sois toute à moi!

à Madame Pauline Viardot

THE BELL
(LA CLOCHE)

VICTOR HUGO
Translated by Arthur Westbrook

(Original Key)

CAMILLE SAINT-SAËNS

Lone____ in thy dark old tow'r V with tur - rets scarred and
Seule____ en ta som - bre tour____ V aux fai - tes den - te -

drear, V Whence thy deep voice de - scends on the roofs clus - t'ring
lés, V D'où ton souf - fle des - cend sur les toits é - bran -

near, V O bell, high o - ver all,____ V 'mid the clouds thou art
lés, V Ô clo - che sus - pen - du - e V au mi - lieu des nu -

hung,__ ⋁ Which so of-ten re-sound ⋁ to thy clam-or-ous tongue._
é-es, ⋁ Par ton vas-te rou-lis ⋁ si sou-vent re-mu-é-

__ ⋁ In shad-ow now thou sleep-est, ⋁ hushed__ is ev'-ry
es, ⋁ Tu dors en ce mo-ment dans l'ombre,__ ⋁ et rien ne

sound, ⋁ In the midst of the dark-ness dwells si-lence pro-
luit Sous ta voû-te pro-fonde où som-meil-le le

meno p

found! Oh!_____ when draws near a
bruit! Oh!_____ tan-dis qu'un es-

soul, V and, tho' no word is spo - ken, V
prit V qui jus - qu'à toi s'é - lan - ce, V

Soars up to thee on high V through si - lence yet un -
Si - len - ci - eux aus - si, V con - tem - ple ton si -

bro - ken, V Dost not some in - stinct feel -
len - ce, V Sens - tu, par cet ins - tinct

Vague - ly bless - ed and dear— V Which must ev - er re -
vague et plein de dou - ceur V Qui ré - vè - le tou -

veal__ that a sis - ter is near?_____ V In this
jours_ u - ne sœur à la sœur,_____ V Qu'à cette

hour of re - pose_____ V when the twi - light is
heure où s'en - dort_____ V la soi - rée ex - pi -

dy - ing, V A soul_____ is near to thee;
ran - te, V Une âme_____ est près de toi,

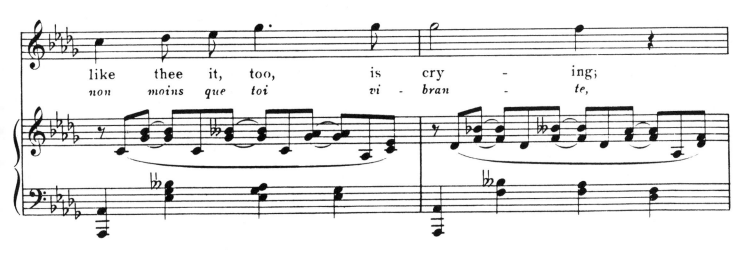

like thee it, too, is cry - ing;
non moins que toi vi - bran - te,

Crying with solemn sound V to the
Qui bien sou-vent aus-si V jette un

blue vault on high, V And doth
bruit so-len-nel, V Et se

mourn in its love e'en as
plaint dans l'a-mour com-me

thou___ V in the sky!___
toi___ V dans le ciel!___

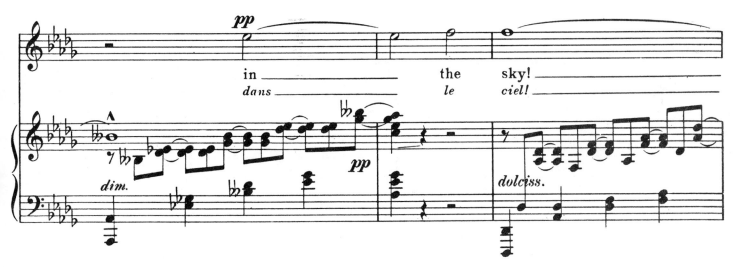

à Madame Marie Barbier

MOONLIGHT
(CLAIR DE LUNE)

(Original Key)

CATULLE MENDÈS
Translated by Isabella G. Parker

CAMILLE SAINT-SAËNS

With-in___ the grove___ so dream-
Dans la___ fo - rêt___ que crée___

- - y wend - ing,___ I walk___
un rê - - ve___ Je vais___

___ at eve___ the for - - est lone.___
___ le soir___ dans la___ fo - rêt;___

Ap - pears ___ thy frail ___ im-age, ___
Ta frèle ___ i - ma - - - ge m'ap-

my own, ___ Be - side me ___ each mo - ment ___
- pa - rait ___ Et che - mine ___ a - vec moi ___

at - tend - - - - ing.
sans trè - - - - ve.

pp

Or is it not thy film - y veil, ___
N'est - ce pas là ton voi - le fin, ___

own ten-der tears? Or can it
ler dou-ce - ment? Ou se peut -

be, as it ap - pears,____ that thou to
il ré - el - le - ment ____ Qu'à mes có -

me art in tears re - turn - - -
tés,__ en__ pleurs, tu vien - - -

ing?
nes?

EVENING
(LE SOIR)

MICHEL CARRÉ
Translated by Isabella G. Parker

(Original Key)

AMBROISE THOMAS

The earth,_____ parched at e - ven, Is
La terre_____ em - bra - sé - e At -

wait - - ing that heav - en The fresh dew may bring._____
tend_____ la ro - sé - e Qui tom - be des cieux._____

Cool - er winds are_____
La cha - leur_____ s'a -

dim. *pp*

blow - ing, Blest_____ re - lief be - stow - ing. The birds sweet - er
pai - se, On_____ res - pire à l'ai - se, L'oi - seau chan - te

poco cresc.

sing, The birds_____ sweet - er sing._____
mieux, L'oi - seau_____ chan - te mieux._____

cresc.
Thro' their veil of splen - - dor Tell love's sto - ry
À tra - vers son voi - - le, Parle aux a - mou -
dim. rit.
sweet, While star - beams ten - der Tell love's sto - ry
reux, Plus d'une é - toi - le Par - - le aux a - mou -
pp
rit.
smorz.
pp
sweet, love's sto - ry sweet, love's sto - ry sweet.
reux, aux a - mou - reux, aux a - mou - reux.
a tempo
8
tr
smorz.

THE SIGH
(SOUPIR)

THÉOPHILE GAUTIER
Translated by Isabella G. Parker

CHARLES WIDOR

From my breast dropt a love - ly flow - ret,___ So
J'ai lais - sé___ de mon sein de nei - ge___ Tom -

bright yet the stream was its grave; A - las! A - las! A -
ber un œil - let rouge à l'eau; Hé - las! Hé - las! Hé -

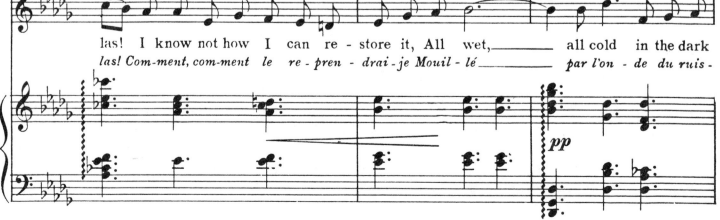

las! I know not how I can re - store it, All wet,___ all cold in the dark
las! Com - ment, com - ment le re - pren - drai - je Mouil - lé___ par l'on - de du ruis -